W9-BMO-050

MOUNTAIN VIEW PUBLIC LIBRARY

1000579760

MOUNTAIN VIEW

PUBL   RARY

Mountain View, Calif.

Monkeys and Other Mammals

MOUNTAIN VIEW
PUBLIC LIBRARY
Mountain View, Calif.

by
Mary Schulte

Children's Press®
A Division of Scholastic Inc.
New York Toronto London Auckland Sydney
Mexico City New Delhi Hong Kong
Danbury, Connecticut

These content vocabulary word builders
are for grades 1-2.

Consultant: Professor Diane Doran
The State University of New York
Stony Brook, New York

Curriculum Specialist: Linda Bullock

Special thanks to Omaha's Henry Doorly Zoo

Photo Credits:

Photographs © 2005: Corbis Images: 9 bottom right (Robert Dowling), 4 bottom left, 9 bottom left (Amos Nachoum), 5 top right, 10 (Dann Tardif/LWA); Minden Pictures: cover left inset, 4 top, 7 (Gerry Ellis), 9 top left (Mitsuaki Iwago), cover background (Konrad Wothe); Peter Arnold Inc.: 23 bottom left (Gerard Lacz), 1, 2, 4 bottom right, 13, 20 bottom (Fritz Polking); Photo Researchers, NY: cover center inset (Daryl Balfour), cover right inset (Alan Carey), 23 top left (W. Treat Davidson), 9 top right (Tim Davis), 5 bottom right, 14, 15 (Gregory G. Dimijian), 5 top left, 16, 17, 21 bottom, 23 top right (Tom & Pat Leeson), 21 top (D. Roberts/SPL); PhotoEdit/Myrleen Ferguson Cate: 19; PictureQuest: 5 bottom left, 11, 20 top (Digital Vision), 23 bottom right (IFA/eStock Photo); Stone/Getty Images/Keren Su: back cover.

Book Design: Simonsays Design!

Library of Congress Cataloging-in-Publication Data

Schulte, Mary, 1958-
 Monkeys and other mammals / by Mary Schulte.
  p. cm. — (Scholastic news nonfiction readers)
 Includes bibliographical references (p.   ) and index.
 ISBN 0-516-24933-9 (lib. bdg.)
 1. Mammals—Juvenile literature. I. Title. II. Series.
 QL706.2.S34 2005
 599—dc22

2005003289

Copyright © 2005 by Scholastic Inc.
All rights reserved. Published simultaneously in Canada.
Printed in the United States of America.
CHILDREN'S PRESS and associated logos are trademarks and or registered trademarks of Scholastic Library Publishing. SCHOLASTIC and associated logos are trademarks and or registered trademarks of Scholastic Inc.

1 2 3 4 5 6 7 8 9 10 R 14 13 12 11 10 09 08 07 06 05

CONTENTS

WORD HUNT

Look for these words as you read. They will be in **bold**.

cheetah
(**chee**-tuh)

mammal
(**mam**-uhl)

monkey
(**muhng**-kee)

fur
(fur)

infant
(**in**-fuhnt)

nursing
(**nur**-sing)

vertebrate
(**vur**-tuh-brate)

Mammals!

Have you ever seen a **cheetah**, a giraffe, or a **monkey**?

All of these animals are **mammals**.

There are lots of ways you can tell an animal is a mammal.

Cheetahs are mammals.

Most mammals give birth to babies.

Baby mammals look like their parents.

Cats have kittens.

Pigs have piglets.

Dogs have puppies.

Whales have calves.

cat and kittens

dog and puppies

whale and calf

pig and piglets

Baby mammals drink their mother's milk.

These mammals are monkeys. A baby monkey is called an **infant**.

The infant is **nursing**. It is feeding on its mother's milk.

Human babies are called infants, too.

human baby

infant

Mammals are warm-blooded.

That means that their body temperature stays the same.

Monkeys are warm-blooded.

If the air is cold, their bodies can stay warm for some time.

Mammals have backbones.

The backbone supports the mammal's body.

Animals with a backbone are called **vertebrates**.

A giraffe has a backbone.

That means giraffes are vertebrates.

backbone

A backbone helps the giraffe stand tall.

All mammals have hair, or **fur**, at some time in their lives.

The hair or fur protects the mammal from the heat and the cold.

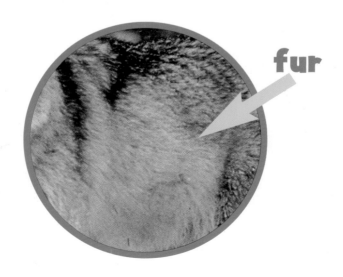

fur

This wolf's fur helps it stay warm in winter.

What kind of animal
are you?

You drank your mother's
milk when you were born.

You are warm-blooded.

You have a backbone.

You have hair.

Guess what?

You are a mammal!

WHAT IS A MAMMAL?

Baby mammals drink their mother's milk.

Mammals are warm-blooded.

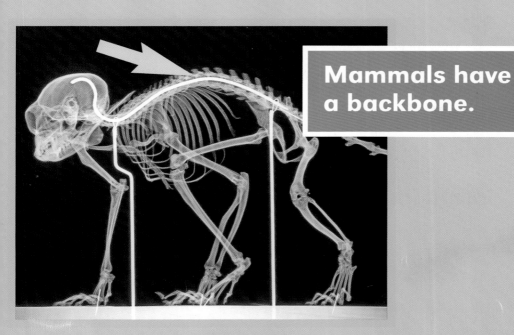

Mammals have a backbone.

All mammals have fur at some time in their lives.

YOUR NEW WORDS

cheetah (**chee**-tuh) a kind of cat that lives in Africa and parts of Asia

fur (fur) a thick coat of hair on mammals

infant (**in**-fuhnt) a baby monkey or baby human

mammal (**mam**-uhl) a warm-blooded animal that nurses its babies

monkey (**muhng**-kee) an animal that is a mammal

nursing (**nur**-sing) feeding a baby mother's milk

vertebrate (**vur**-tuh-brate) an animal with a backbone

IS IT A MAMMAL?

Alligator
(No. It's a reptile.)

Eagle
(No. It's a bird.)

Python
(No. It's a reptile.)

Shark
(No. It's a fish.)

23

INDEX

FIND OUT MORE

Book:
DK Guide to Mammals by Ben Morgan
(Dorling Kindersley Limited, 2003)

Website:
http://members.enchantedlearning.com/subjects/mammals/

MEET THE AUTHOR:

Mary Schulte is a newspaper photo editor and author of books and articles for children. She is the author of the other animal classification books in this series. She lives in Kansas City, Missouri, and her favorite mammals are her children Sarah, Daniel, and Solomon.